Where's the Baby?

Where's the Baby?

by TOM PAXTON
illustrated by MARK GRAHAM

Morrow Junior Books
NEW YORK

The text type is 18-point Galliard.
Oil on Strathmore bristol paper was used for the full-color artwork.

Printed in Hong Kong by South China Printing Company (1988) Ltd.
1   2   3   4   5   6   7   8   9   10

Library of Congress Cataloging-in-Publication Data
Paxton, Tom.
Where's the baby? / by Tom Paxton ; illustrated by Mark Graham.
p.   cm.
Summary: After looking for the baby in various spots, the reader
finds her in a very safe place.
ISBN 0-688-10692-7.—ISBN 0-688-10693-5 (lib. bdg.)
[1. Babies—Fiction.   2. Stories in rhyme.]   I. Graham, Mark ill.   II. Title.
PZ8.3.P2738Wh   1993   [E]—dc20   92-39875   CIP   AC

To my daughters, Jennifer and Kate
T. P.

To Madeline Eliza
M. G.

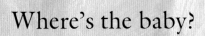

Where's the baby?

In the car?
Is she traveling very far?
Sitting there in her own car seat?
Honking her horn on Maple Street?
Trying to make the big car go?
Is she in the car now?

NO!
Where's the baby?
Where, oh, where?
Is she sitting in her high chair?
Having dinner, filling her cup?
Smacking her lips, eating it up?
Dinner's over, doesn't she know?
Is she in her high chair?

NO!
Where's the baby?
Let's explore.
Is she playing down on the floor?
Is she banging on pots and pans?
Building a wall of pea-soup cans?
Trying to see how high they'll go?
Is she in the kitchen?

NO!
Where's the baby?
Can you see?
Is she as busy as can be?
Hammering, rattling, singing songs?
Is she trying to sing along?
Humming tunes with the radio?
Is she in her playpen?

NO!
Where's the baby?
Tell me where!
Is she playing with Teddy Bear?
Dressing him for a Teddy walk?
Telling him tales in Teddy talk?
Teddy loves good stories, you know.
Is she with her Teddy?

NO!
Where's the baby?
Where's she now?
Doing a puzzle of a cow?
Finding the pieces one by one
Till finally she gets it done?
Is she getting the cow to show,
Filling in the puzzle?

NO!
Where's the baby?
Well, let's look!
Is she reading a picture book?
Turning the pages, having fun?
That big book is her favorite one.
Snuggled up in the chair just so,
Is she reading stories?

NO!
Where's the baby?
Well, let's see.
Is she sitting on Daddy's knee?
Is she watching the fire blaze?
Hearing about the olden days?
Things were different long ago.
Is she with her daddy?

NO!
Where's the baby?
In the tub?
Does she like to "rub-a-dub-dub"?
Is she playing with bathtub toys
And making lots of bathtub noise?
Splashing, laughing, loving it so.
Is she in the bathtub?

NO!
Where's the baby?
Where's she gone?
Is she putting her nightgown on?
Soft and comfy, warm and snug,
Is it time for a bedtime hug?
Is she where the sleepy heads go,
Putting on her nightgown?

NO!
Where's the baby?
I declare.
Is she upstairs brushing her hair?
Hair so soft and fluffy and fine;
Gently brushing to make it shine?
She loves to tie it with a bow.
Is she upstairs brushing?

NO!
Where's the baby?
She's nearby.
Listening to a lullaby.
Nestled in a bed just her size;
Now she's ready to close her eyes.
Slowly nodding her sleepy head.
Where's the baby?

Safe in bed!

5